SELF-DISCIPLINE

*FIND OUT HOW TO ANALYZE PEOPLE,
INFLUENCE PEOPLE, AND MANIPULATE
PEOPLE USING EMOTIONAL INTELLIGENCE
WITH POWERFUL COMMUNICATION AND
PERSUASION*

Bob Gutierrez

TABLE OF CONTENTS

INTRODUCTION

Self-discipline is the most necessary and beneficial skill every person possesses. This ability is essential in every place of life, and although most humans acknowledge its importance, very few do anything to reinforce it.

Contrary to popular belief, self-discipline does not mean being harsh towards oneself or having a limited, restrictive lifestyle. Self-discipline skills are self-control, which indicates internal power and management of yourself, your actions, and your reactions. Self-discipline provides you with the ability to stick to your choices and comply with them without changing your mind and is, therefore, one of the essential requirements to accomplish goals. Possession of this talent allows you to complete them with your selection and plans until you achieve them. It also manifests as inner strength, helping you overcome addictions, laxity, and laziness and help you comply with whatever you do. Self-discipline benefits and importance

Self-discipline benefit self-discipline is one of the most essential and valuable abilities we should all possess.

This talent is unavoidable in every place of life, and although most humans are well aware of its importance, very few do something to beef it up.

Contrary to what is often believed, self-discipline is no longer rigid towards itself or inhabited by limited, restrictive lifestyles. Self-discipline is the ability to control self-control, which indicates inner strength and how to manage yourself, your actions, and your reactions. Self-discipline empowers you to stick to your decisions and follow through them, causing a change in your mind, and therefore, is one of the essential requirements for accomplishing goals.

Possession of this ability allows you to carry out your selections and plans until you complete them.

It also manifests as inner strength, supporting you to overcome addictions, senescence, and laziness and comply with everything you do.

Build strong willpower and self-discipline. Follow strong willpower and self-discipline: practice and practice to build your willpower, self-discipline, and inner strength.

Learn to overcome laxity and laziness and promote decisiveness, perseverance, and inner strength.

One of its key traits is the ability to reject instant gratification and happiness in favor of some higher benefit that requires effort and time to achieve.

CHAPTER 1

Know your weaknesses

This is a detailed interview of how you are sure to answer in any way... are your weaknesses? There is usually the temptation to take something that is not a weak spot and makes you feel good. "Oh, sometimes I think I'm too punctual."

This is not what employers are looking for. Everyone has their weaknesses, even the world's most prominent CEO, and acknowledging and correcting these weaknesses is the real key to success. If you sit there in your interview and act as you are, the recruiter will see it right.

So how do you understand what your weaknesses are? And how do you increase them? These steps below help you to correct those flaws and address them appropriately.

Think about your career

The first aspect of doing this is what capabilities you need. I mean, I'm doing garbage in math, but seeing that my job involves writing all day doesn't speak honestly. Similarly, there is no point in stressing about the reality that your grammar will not be up to scratch when your work is in all numbers and spreadsheets.

Once you know what kind of abilities you need, move yourself to a reasonably tall look, and find out what commands you, master. People regularly throw buzzwords such as communication, teamwork, management, and interpersonal skills into a job application, but you stop and assume if you possess these skills.

Think about the comments you have received, whether in school or university or as a team stage. If a man has called you for something, what was it for once? It is natural to get protection about such an element and effort and blame someone else, but often you can ignore some part of your behavior that is also at fault.

You likely desire to try to trust one in addition to this - it may want to become a friend, household member, or tutor - if they can (creatively) point out some weaknesses for you. An external opinion usually helps.

Some different questions you might want to ask:

- What duties do you leave until you finish last on your to-do list?
- What is your energy
- When do you need help?
- All of these help you portray a genuine and honest picture of yourself that you can actively improve.

Hard vs. soft

And no, now we will not talk about Brexit here. All abilities can be divided into hard and tender skills. A challenging ability is a sensible talent, such as participating in an instrument or coding. A gentle power is extra summative and tied to your personality, so things like communication, emotional brain, and management will all fall under the category of smooth abilities.

In short, the most difficult competencies can be learned through anyone, although they will likely take a proper portion of time and dedication, while gentle competencies are more intimately connected to your innate personality, and if you do, Then it is more difficult to increase. T naturally possesses that skill. Classifying your weaknesses into hard and soft abilities will help you correctly understand a diagram of action to enhance them.

Take a personality test

The world of character tests is problematic and complex to navigate. What is legal, and what is not? The Myers – Brigade personality test is best considered, although it has been referred to as valid, and the investigation of Big Five personality features is now more frequently referred to. This is your personality's value in 5 key areas: openness, conscientiousness, extroversion, agreeableness, and insanity; You give one percentage point in each.

While you should take a pinch of salt along the way because some tick box questions no longer accurately represent someone's personality, they are an accurate way of telling you about your character and how you react to positive things.

How to rotate weaknesses

Once you establish your weaknesses and what capabilities are quintessential for the industry you choose, you want to turn these weaknesses into strengths. If you lack a problematic skill - coding, for example - nothing is stopping you from learning right now. The soft ability can be tricky, though; If you are an introvert, you will likely go to war with public speeches or interpersonal skills.

If you are conscious of your weaknesses, you have already taken the first vital step to address them, although in some cases, you can do as much work as possible to ensure your weaknesses, which Prevents you from going to work.

Agreement with the organization.

If you are not good at raising your opinion in meetings or providing your work to the team, then put as much ton as possible on the rise to make it happen.

You need to work harder to fill your skill gaps.

Practice Makes Perfect. It's easy to get away from things you don't do so confidently, but the more you try it, the more you will achieve. If you are afraid of networking, the only way you can improve yourself is to keep yourself there and run it.

Use the people around you. If you can understand your weakness, then there is no insult in calling humans around you to help you. Look at the humans on your team, and if there is someone you believe will do more in performing a unique task than you, ask them to supply you a hand.

Many human beings tend to concentrate fully on their powers and make their efforts to improve these qualities as much as possible.

It is not uncommon to discover anyone who is honestly afraid to face their weaknesses and flaws, so they indeed bury them in a box and ignore them as much as possible.

When it comes to an individual's improvement, they need to discover their weaknesses if they wish to develop and enhance their full potential.

Knowing your weaknesses is as important as understanding your strengths. These weaknesses that you often try to leave aside may limit you from almost chasing after your goals and accomplishing many significant matters in your life. However, the right thing about weaknesses is that you can improve them.

The enjoyable way for you to find out your weaknesses is to take a pen and paper and start by writing all the matters that scare you or stop you.

Before you go into detail and start choosing positive weaknesses, make sure you write about all the things that are the object of a problem in your everyday life.

For example, you can write about how you dislike being around new humans or how you become sluggish at work for a few days and cannot finish on time. The last step for you is to reduce those weaknesses, such as being shy or being lazy.

After you finish writing them all, go ahead and select the five you think to represent the most to your personality. These are the five weaknesses that are probably bringing you back to your everyday life and who want the most improvement.

1. It can make you stronger

Weaknesses can leave us behind and make us see ourselves in a very prone and weak way. Most of the time, though, it is no longer what we are, and we can exchange a lot of matters in our lives if we consider ourselves.

Working towards finding your weaknesses and improving them can help you gain some needed strength in many components of your life. You will be able to address problems much less complicated, and you will be able to understand that no one trusts what your path is that you will be able to pull successfully.

You will also be able to go ahead and do things that would typically be out of your comfort zone, such as being inspected for a job you've always wanted or talking to a specific person you never dared.

Was not. Discovering your weaknesses and rounding them up can provide you with a new outlook on existence and help free you from the things that would usually hold you back.

2. It can help you focus on improving yourself

Understanding and acknowledging your weaknesses can be an enjoyable way for you to start working towards growing yourself. Most of the time, we are the only ones who hold back from pursuing and pursuing themselves after their dreams.

It is a satisfying way to start working on yourself and improve yourself to depend on those to make you happy.

Even though it may be a child step compared to others, it may just be the growth you want to start taking higher and essential steps closer to improving yourself and growing a new lifestyle for you.

3. It can help you fight mental illness

A person who focuses solely on their weaknesses is often fragile and lacks the motivation to do something meaningful to change their life. These humans are certainly not aware of their shortcomings, although they usually trust that they have some weaknesses rather than some disadvantages.

This causes their arrogance to diminish significantly, and they feel utterly immaculate for doing anything. To flip this situation around, you have to go ahead and list your weaknesses on paper. Be it a man or a woman that you believe. Go through this list and tell you which people are exactly there and which are not.

Helping anyone who knows you need to help you understand that you are too harsh on yourself and want to get out of this challenging cycle. When you start working on these weaknesses and start doing something about them completely, you will see that your temperament will grow, and you will move towards intellectual health problem, which is bothering you and keeping you back Has been

4. It can help you get yourself a higher version

One of the essential things to keep thinking is that no one is ideal, and no one starts as successful and confident. It takes time to emerge as both of these things consistently, and to get there, a man or woman will have to do the challenging work to understand themselves better and focal points to make all their weaknesses strengths.

While having a weakness is not bad, it can turn into a hassle when the person spends too much time focusing on them and investigating all the events that their flaws might hold them back. It is essential that you consistently achieve and understand your weaknesses but also work on improving them to maintain the existence you dream of.

I focus too much on details

Being "detail-oriented" is a good thing in general, although it can also be considered a weakness if you are someone who tends to spend a great deal of time on the specifics of a project.

Be sure to explain how you are growing in this area by looking at the big picture. Even though employers may no longer like the idea of being an employee who is predetermined with the best points, a candidate who fines and tries for consistency can be a fantastic asset.

Example: "My best weakness is that now and then, I do a lot of tones on the small print of an undertaking at the center point and spend too much time analyzing the delicate issues. I am trying to pose a danger in this area at daily intervals to check with myself and refocus myself on the more excellent picture. That way, I can still catch some great barring in small print so that it affects my productivity or team's ability to meet deadlines. "

I have a hard time completing a project

When you spend an arrear of time and effort on something, it is easy to be concerned about marking it whole or passing it on to every other team. There is always room for improvement, and some people over-criticize their work or try to make last-minute changes, which can threaten the timeline.

At the same time, however, last-minute opinions can help remove errors and make for a more sophisticated finished product.

If this is your weakness, share that you are trying to improve by giving yourself a closing date for all modifications and being proactive about the changes to no longer wait until the last minute.

Example: "My biggest weakness is that I let a project go through a difficult time now and then. I am the most prominent critic of my work, and I can consistently find something that wants to be enhanced or changed. To help improve me in this area, I give myself deadlines for amendments. This helps ensure that I am no longer revising the closing minute.

I have trouble saying, "no."

Helping colleagues take the initiative and better manage their workload is a sufficient balance.

From an employer's point of view, anyone who accepts all requests looks committed and eager - but there can be anyone who doesn't understand their limits and is supportive or cut-off to end their job. It Eliminates the need for date extensions.

If you are anyone eager to do new tasks, you cannot deliver yourself to say "no," you better self-organize by organizing your duties and setting more sensible expectations. How to manage yourself by working around yourself as well.

Example: "My biggest weak position is that I have trouble requesting again and declaring not to take more than I can handle." In the past, it has made me feel careless or burned. To help improve me in this area, I use a challenge management app to imagine a vast job at any other number, and I can understand that I have more to take. Whether there is the bandwidth for. "

I get impatient when projects go beyond the deadline

When expressing external stress or frustration over an overlooked deadline, a weakness can be seen, with employers being workers who value closing dates and consciously try to take the initiative within the time frame.

If you use this as a weakness of your job interview, focus your answer on how you admire the work done on time, and improve the processes to perform the task efficiently. So you are increasing your support.

Example: "My most significant weak spot is that I get impatient when projects run before the deadline. I am a sticker for due dates and get uncomfortable when the work is not executed on time. To avoid this, I have started to be more proactive and pay for interest in reacting to positive and supporting motivational and supportive efficiency. "

I should use more rides ...

Each candidate will have areas to improve their expertise. Perhaps it is something specific like building a pivot table in Excel, or maybe it is a skill like math, writing, or public speaking. Whatever it is, sharing what you wish to enhance shows the interviewer that you are self-aware and like to challenge yourself. However, make sure that you will not respond with a weakness that is unavoidable for the role.

Some of the common areas humans require experience:

- Oral communication
- written communication
- team leadership
- Analysis explained
- Representative work
- Provide optimistic criticism

Specific package (i.e., "I would like to improve my PowerPoint presentation skills.")

I sometimes lack confidence

Lack of self-confidence is a general weakness, especially among entry-level contributors. Disabilities in their work may at once experienced a lack of self-assurance. For example, you may also feel unworthy to speak at an important meeting when your perception may help the crew get around.

Being polite when working with others can be helpful, and maintaining a positive amount of self-confidence is very important to get your work done to the last level.

If this is the weak point you choose to present in your interview, then emphasize why you believe, appreciate the price you provide, and the attitude you have confidence in your business place. Have practiced showing (even when you can't always feel it).

Example: "In the past, I struggled with confidence on the spot.

It has been beneficial for me to maintain the jogging file of the impact I have made on my crew and my organization, so I must be confident of the high skills and unique talent that I deliver to the table.

I have also made it a point to voice my thoughts and opinions during meetings when I think they are fantastic and add a fee to the conversation. Because of this, our crew ended up adopting my concept for a new financing process, resulting in a 10% reduction in the time it takes to format our annual budget. "

I may have trouble asking for help

Asking for help is a fundamental skill when you lack expertise in a positive space and get burned out or cannot manage your workload. Knowing when and how to ask for help reflects self-awareness and helps a corporation advance a viable disability. Being a solid work ethic and having practical qualities of being fair, it should be more for the enterprise to know when to seek help.

If you are aware that it is difficult to ask for help in the past, explain why you recognize that it is beneficial and the efforts you have made to enhance this skill.

Example: "Because I am impartial and I talk about working quickly, when I wanted to, it became difficult for me to ask for help.

I have learned that it is a good deal more recommended for me and the business I do when I no longer recognize anything or experience burnt by my workload. I also accept that I have many experts who have unique knowledge and skills to improve my work. Although I am working on it, I can still do a lot of good work to help those around me. "

It has been hard for me to work with a specific personality

Even the most bending people may have trouble working with others who have specific characteristics or personality traits. Along with having the ability to do real teamwork, you have a strong awareness of how you work with others and change your strategy to serve the organization better.

If this has been your weak spot in the past, explain the character types you have had trouble working with, and rapidly identify intentions as to why.

Then discuss ways that have simultaneously adjusted your communication or work style to work better towards a common purpose.

Example: "In the past, I have found it challenging to work with aggressive character types.

When I push the limits in personalities, it makes an enterprise stronger.

I soothe my very thoughts and opinions round-the-clock. To fight this, I have made it a factor to spend extra time with colleagues I feel uncomfortable working with. By gaining additional knowledge about them, their communication style, and their inspirations, I can collaborate with these character types so that we can each equally contribute our strengths and skills. "

It can be challenging for me to maintain a healthy work/life balance

Finding work/life stability is essential to maintain motivation in your job. While this is only respectable and indicates a strong work ethic for spending your time and power at work, it is imperative to prioritize spending time with your family, hobbies, vacation, or relaxing.

By doing this, you can feel refreshed during labor and help with motivation, creativity, and a high-quality approach.

If this is the weak point that you select for existing on some level in your interview, then explain how you have made it a factor to find a balance between survival and work, and as a result, you have changed your position. How to increase You can also explain the work/life stability, something you find important in the role for which you are applying. Before presenting as an example, you should do significant research about employer culture.

If you are interviewing for a task in which your smartphone needs to be on and working at all times, you probably would not say that you flip your cellphone at night for the remainder of your work/life.

Example: "Because I just love my job and have ambitious career goals, it can be difficult for me to maintain a healthy balance between work and my personal life.

When I sidelined my non-public needs, I saw a terrible impact on my motivation and a focal point.

As a result, I have made it a factor to create space in my schedule and spend time with my family.

During dinner time, it is helpful to do small activities like putting your smartphone on silent. When I have a delicate work/life balance, I have noticed that my production is of high quality, I can finish more work, and I am excited to come to work in the morning. "

In the past, I have been uncomfortable with ambiguity

Many jobs require candidates who are happy to define my tasks and work towards goals. This skill should give them experience, consideration, and accountability with ambiguity in the workplace. While it is undoubtedly beneficial to follow precise instructions carefully, it is also excellent to determine what it takes to achieve the preferred result.

If this is the weakness you are presenting in an interview, achieve success, which you have found in the following directions, but your career is also admirable when searching for relief with ambiguity. You should also explain the steps you are taking to define your workday when given unclear duties or goals.

Example: "In my final role as a marketing intern, I determined that my supervisor gave exact instructions about my responsibilities.

Because I became familiar with having a healthy direction, I become uncertain when drawing near a vague project or goal.

It is my goal not to emerge with ambiguity as an entirely blissful but successful work.

To do this, I have created a personal framework for times when I feel overwhelmed or careless through a vague undertaking that involves conducting structured research and asking a concerned number of professionals for advice. Doing this helped me when working on ambiguous tasks or close to less specific or defined goals.

CHAPTER 2

Remove temptations.

Are you desirable to resist temptation? We all fall prey to little temptation now and then, but some humans have more willpower than others. The attraction is about the need for something that is often not right or good for you. Usually, the temptation urges you to fulfill your desires in the short term without thinking about what might happen later. [1] Unfortunately, tricks can additionally turn into obsessions. You can feel dissatisfied, guilty, or upset by giving in to temptation. Learn how to respond to temptation and increase your self-control.

Recognize manageable temptation.

The temptation is all about self-control, and greed situations are often about the conflict between chance satisfaction and long-term goals. [2] For example, if you are on a diet, you may also be tempted to eat a tasty cheesecake piece, evicting you from the daily case.

The temptation for instant gratification and eating cheesecake will result. However, giving will also interfere with your long-term goal of converting to extra healthy by keeping high sugar foods.

As with any other example, if you are already in a relationship, get information about people who might be tempted to cheat on you.

These people may also be old sails that have come back into your life, coworkers, or the people you interact with within a personal setting.

However, the temptation is not consistently apparent. For example, suppose you are a business expert, and you have an attraction to knock a few days a month early on a Friday afternoon. A couple of early departures does not appear like a big deal, but it should indicate to your agency that you cannot be trusted with responsibility for long-term dreams such as endangering goods and advancement. Should be put

Remove yourself from temptation. You also want to stay away from people you usually smoked.

If you are tempted to drink, the bar's annual work celebration will likely assign your determination. Be alert for understandable temptations and stay away from them when possible. In this way, you cannot be a closed-guard, and you will usually organize to deal with temptations.

If you cannot altogether remove yourself from a situation or person, try manipulating the problem so that it is more difficult to act on your temptation. For example, if you are tempted to cheat with a friend, avoid one-on-one situations. Always meet in a group, if you want to see the person.

Be honest. If you refuse something or someone who is tempting you, do not blame him, or you want to lie. Be truthful about why you deny something. This can support your resolve in the future and may even reduce temptation.

For example, if you are tempted to cheat and the man or woman you want to ask, actually refuse it by saying that you are already in a relationship. Once she realizes this, it may be a lot less possible for her to flirt with you in the future.

Imagine yourself resisting temptation.

In this approach, photograph yourself accepting or touching the trick before putting yourself down and walking away from it. Imagine this ride in as many elements as you can.

Once you have practiced enough, you can also deliberately try to cope with temptation.

Go to keep and face your temptation. [4] This technique is no longer terrible for addictions, such as drug or alcohol addictions. The visualization of giving or contact with the paradox can act as a trigger and make resistance to this temptation very difficult.

Think about the long-term results. When you favor something, it is convenient to consider instant gratification. You will hurt your partner, you will trust that person, and you can also lose the relationship. However, we are all the time engaged in what researchers call "epsilon-cost inducements," or these small cases that do not seem consequential on their own but add up to more considerable outcomes. People are regularly having a hard time denying these temptations because they appear so modest.

For example, attempting a single cigarette or eating a single piece of cheesecake is unlikely to result in immediate, long-term, substantial terrible consequences.

However, cigarette smoking makes you more likely to have one and all the other, which will increase your general risk of adverse effects. And even a single cigarette can cause immediate damage to your body and increase the risk of diseases like cancer.

Try to reflect on your moves in a broader context. Not a single slice of cheesecake will kill you. Although it will be healthier if you are trying to keep away from sugar, it will protect you from that long-term goal. Excess calories will additionally increase over time if you continue to give in. Thinking of matters in this way, as an alternative to private events, can improve self-control.

You may also find that imagining long-term fines can help you build your resistance. For example, if you are tempted to smoke, imagine yourself as the most cancer patient for chemotherapy. Imagine how terrible you feel, how expensive your treatments have become, and how heart-breaking your family is.

Distract yourself.

Sometimes, fixing what is tempting, you can make it more difficult to resist.

Instead, Lookup has proven that distracting yourself with the help of something exciting or enhancing your idea can help in the temptation of a fight.

You can try to meditate, do yoga, go for a jog, or connect with friends. Whatever you do to distract yourself, throw yourself completely into it.

You may also like to do something that pairs you with others who want help. Focus your interest away from those people who will respect you. It can take your mind away from attachment.

Having a specific "distraction plan" is a desirable idea. For example, tell yourself that you will get up and leave for a while if you know the cigarettes' urge.

Do not supply yourself with a choice. If you are tempted with the help of something, do not give in to your self-belief that you have the desire to provide or stay away from it. If you take precedence over the situation, you must reject whatever tempts you.

For example, if you feel the temptation to cheat on your partner, avoid flirting with an interested colleague. Since you recognize that you do not choose to cheat, do not do anything that interests you.

As in every other example, if you are struggling to stay on the low-sugar consumption plan given to you using your doctor, you should refuse to invite holiday events that might be sweet and full of fatty foods. However, this option also limits your ability to socialize and interact with others, reflecting on whether this is the path you want to take.

Make concrete plans Create a deliberate graph for yourself, such as "I will no longer order cheesecakes at lunch so that I can stay in tune with my healthier consumption habits. I'll have an apple" or "I'll only have one beer." Tonight's birthday celebration and asking my partner to remind me to go to another one. "Announcement of these plans for myself in concrete, specific phrase immediate satisfaction

Than the person who can help you focus on your long-term goals.

It can be helpful to formulate your plans in phrases of "if-then." For example, you might come up with this scenario: "If I am provided with a piece of cake at a party, I will say 'No, thanks, I'm staring at my sugar," and closed by someone Start a dialogue with done. "

Build your competencies through practice. Many research studies have shown that you, as an adult, can also power through training. These workout routines increase extra efficiency and reduce your impulsivity. Like your physical muscles, the strength of your muscles will also improve with advancing exercise.

One way to exercise is to try to trade or spoil a habit, even a trivial one. Therefore, if you know that you continuously brush the enamel starting on the proper aspect of your mouth, make up your mind to start on the left element instead.

Scheduling each day's activities is another correct method of practice. For example, you probably create a design to get up at 7:30 am each day, along with the weekend, and eat a cooked breakfast as an alternative to donut grab. As you adopt this routine, you can increase your brain skills.

You can also try to practice willpower in additional meaningful ways, such as choosing a bike to go to school twice a week instead of driving. Setting dreams and then getting yourself into dependency will help you build your self-discipline "muscle."

Keep an eye on your strength at the energy level of the mind. Like physical energy, self-control can be used. When you exercise, you reach a factor where your muscle tissue is exhausted, and it will be challenging for you to continue to lift or carry those weights. When you practice your decision-making skills, the same factor happens in your brain.

One found out that college students who had to practice willpower in a challenge later more imperfect on the strength of the mind challenges than students who did not flex those self-discipline "muscles" before the activity. So, if you are going to a vacation party with lots of sweets that you want to resist, make sure you don't have lunch in the breakroom near that open container of donuts. This constant stress must wear you down to withstand temptation.

Know the same about this; that decision-making can affect your brain's ability. If you know that you are going into a state of affairs, you need to decide, such as a high-pressure meeting at work, to keep away from other situations on the day you need to resist the temptation. For example, maybe don't say a mass birthday party in the evening, if you know that you have to make some decisions earlier in the day.

Eat well. Eating habits can be a great source of temptation, but healthy eating habits can also help you avoid undermining your resources' strength. One person found that college students who did not eat these days were worse at a willful task than students who had been eating recently and had persistent blood sugar levels.

Even a quick snack, such as a glass of lemonade or a slice of fruit, can help complete your glucose steps and improve your self-control.

Eating foods high in fiber, such as beans, oats, potatoes, and vegetables, will help your glucose phases stay stable rather than dipping or spiking. They also take longer to digest, which will help you feel fuller for longer and help you cope with the temptation of food.

If we have discovered nothing else from the latest place of political indiscretion, we understand this: resisting temptation can be exceptionally challenging.

For me, chocolate is my Achilles' heel.

I know, now not nearly as exciting or malleable, but it is sometimes a hassle.

What I love about chocolate makes me very friendly and happy.

The world must end, though if I have chocolate, everything is fine. At least, temporarily.

I can justify it for a while, although soon, I'm getting some delicious chocolate snack almost every day. I crave it. I choose it, even though I understand that it is not appropriate for me to do it for a long time. Granted, I know how the body and brain work. This is not always rocket science, but it sure takes someday. I know that you conserve your weight when your energy is consumed = calories burned. If you consume more than what you burn, you gain weight. If you eat less, you lose. This is easier on a biological level. Two, but it is exceptionally challenging to implement and achieve.

Blame it on the brain?

I always struggle with this purpose - it is a matter of my mind. Like. In truth, we are both one of a variety of causes. Why here

· Whenever I eat chocolate, I instruct my talent that this is a necessary action - to interest and repeat something. If I do this once, my talent will no longer say honestly, and I cannot yearn for chocolate. However, even if I repeat this action for a few days, my talent will start cramping for chocolate. As it happens, my mind refrains from wildly shouting, "chocolate, chocolate, chocolate!" And I now urge this gut to eat some chocolate. What's worse, the more I eat chocolate, the more regularly it becomes and becomes highly cranky. As time passes, my brain starts eating chocolate as an example, and I feel that I am craving it day and night.

This seems quite unfair. Enjoy a snack with any regularity, and your brain fulfills it and craves you more. Clearly, in an evolutionary sense, one experiences why my intellect would do this. Delightful affairs are preferred since they keep us alive, and food is no exception. It is a spontaneous drive mediated through the hypothalamus and other components of the brain. Darwin would be happy to see my brain function. But I don't. From the point of view of a woman trying to enjoy some chocolate, this is a suggested trick.

So what am I to do? Frankly, I have to train my intelligence on what is important to me to substitute for me as a hindrance. It is no longer enough for me to favor separation; I have to work differently without any doubt. The only way my brain will respond to how it reacts and what it produces is primarily based on what I do - and, in particular, how I focus my attention.

Luckily, I already recognize how to change my brain. I have achieved this before, and I can do it again. I only have to follow the four steps that my mentor and I have developed and outlined in our new ebook, and You Are Not Your Brain. It seems simple, although I know from the ride that it is not. In truth, it takes dedication and effort - as well as time. This is where I have my inspiration and intention, especially for things.

Entry Limit: Whenever possible, I keep the exit material out of the house with me! I have found from travel that if chocolate or other iconic incurable snacks are no longer easily accessible, then I probably would not go to extraordinary lengths to buy them.

Use the 15-minute rule: Don't commit to giving for 15 minutes. See if the craving is even after 15 minutes. If it is, then I try to wait every 15 minutes. I remind myself that longing will pass.

Stop and reflect before you answer: I ask myself, what am I going to do and why? Is this right now going to serve and support a cause honestly, or will I feel sorry about it later?

Remember Biology: I remind myself that every time I consume chocolate, I make the brain's circuitry better and more intense, making it harder to resist cravings in the future.

When any person confesses or is caught in the case of one of the first cases, they say something is affected by saying, "I didn't make it clear." Or "He/she was nothing to me." In one area, they did not want to be in any way. Most people do not desist from cheating on their spouse. It all starts small. It begins with the belief that goes unopposed, perhaps even nurtured in a fantasy. Those thoughts develop into an attitude, and then the mind-brain grows into nature. This dispute erodes boundaries and clouds our sense of right and wrong.

This is challenging for most men. Our DNA is pre-loaded with a solid instinct for experience appeal and desire, but lifestyle and morality demand that we manipulate these instincts. So how do we do that? For our marriages, relationships, or merely spiritual well-being, we need to find out the answer. You are in a fight against sexual temptations, and it is essential to winning them quickly. Here are ten ways to combat sexual attraction.

1. Avoid Tempering Situation

You are winning the initial ability to stay away from the trap. The final aspect that you like to do is discovered by yourself with the object of your unhealthy desires, whether it is photos or real people or not. If contact with that person is necessary, make sure that it is always in a public house, and others are around—set boundaries around your phone, computer, and T.V. Look for a partner who is willing to assist you with accountability.

2. Consider the result

While considering the object of your desire, additionally give some thought to the consequences of the action. Is it going to help or harm your marriage? If she knew how your spouse would respond? Think of a place where you can do tricks, and then think of your wife. Are you in favor of dealing with the consequences? Always think of abandoned games. Where do you want to go? Are your thoughts and movements leading you there?

3. Avoid Pornography

Apart from the apparent motives that turning off porn will help move towards lust, there are psychological objectives. Porn creates unrealistic expectations and brings our minds closer to our spouse. It concentrates your sexual desires outside the domestic and can lead to a path of utter destruction.

4. Use social media with caution

We have reconnected with our earlier people and are familiar with those who are new. For a married person, this can be exceptionally dangerous. Always be alert to the real intentions when using social media.

5. Question your intention

Most of the time, when our mind wanders sexually, we do not just seek pure sex. We are looking for something lacking in our lives and our relationships. It may additionally be that we are trying to distract ourselves from dealing with something difficult. For every man, these matters will be outstanding for his experiences. Locate the root issue and work to correct it.

6. Practice Sexual Intimacy

When there was newness in your relationship, there is no way to feel how you feel; there are many ways to improve this. Improvements in communication, date nights, passionate kisses, and thoughtful gestures are just a few examples. When our mind and heart are occupied in the proper place, there is little space to conduct sexual lust.

7. Constant Prayer

Prayer is the act of speaking your thoughts, concerns, hopes, and desires before God. Take up the desires you are feeling and ask for help. God has created you and knows you and can supply you time and again.

8. Choose Your Friends Wisely

While struggling with sexual temptation, there are plenty of humans to figure out who will inspire and allow it.

9. Keep a high standard

There is a choice to become a gentleman. A very desirable option and there are many more desires in this world these days. Despite the enormous amount of temptation that throws away our volume of life, we must hold ourselves to the highest moral standards levels. Self-discipline in all areas of our lifestyle produces impressive results.

10. Redirect Your Passion

Instead of being managed with the help of untamed lust, direct in that high-quality direction. Use the power you can bless your wife to brainstorm about attitudes. Perhaps the focal point on matters that would make the world better, like volunteering in a homeless shelter. Coach the youth sports team. Mentor harassed individuals.

Temptations are everywhere - the temptation to snack, to go through your workout, to buy impulsively, or to hit the snooze button just one extra time. Here are some cases that you can face with many types of temptation:

Forget the phrase "it can't be." This term can have an incredibly significant (and often negative) effect on our mood in a decision. Instead, "don't" or "don't win." You are getting something rather than denying yourself. It is not that you cannot eat sweets with lunch; you do not eat sweets.

Add others. Work to bring healthy behavior to meetings with your colleagues or go to a fitness class with friends. When the humans of your existence are also concerned about healthy choices, it can be less difficult to stop the temptation than attempting to overcome them.

Keep away the temptation of food. Do you understand the phrase "out of sight, out of mind"? When you cannot see them and are not receptive to them, it is easy to keep away from goodness and behavior. At home, maintain food in the pantry or cupboards alternately at the counter. If there are sweets or banquets at work or home, place them in containers or boxes you cannot see.

Consider your schedule. If your after-work activities are unpredictable and fluctuating during the day, chances are you are tempted repeatedly to pass your evening exercises to accommodate other activities.

If that sounds like you, try to do your first workout in the morning or during lunch.

That way, you will be tempted to pass it in the evening. Do what makes the most experience for your schedule.

Plan. If you are trying to have a morning snack, or have a morning snack, be tempted to learn about what you can do before sleeping at night. Set your exercise clothes, or sleep in them. Mix the elements of your breakfast and make your kitchen clean. It can be tempting later if planning in advance is a little easier.

Remove attachment Sometimes, the temptation is too challenging to pass. When this happens, get rid of it. If you often like to eat ice cream before going to bed, do not buy ice cream. It is simple to resist temptation when giving it will be inconvenient.

To distract. When you entice yourself to do something that goes against your fitness goals, find a higher distraction. It works well if the distraction is something you enjoy and can do or believe anywhere. If you can focus on something different from your temptation, then you cannot start properly.

Make the most of your morning. You have not managed this consistently when you can use your mornings to prevent potential temptations.

Make stuff ahead of time, an exercise in the morning, do you go grocery shopping in the morning, walk your dog - do the cases you can pass on in any other case if you wanted to wait until later.

Come up with the option. In this case, anticipate your temptations as triggers. If you are tempted to have a donut for breakfast, find a healthy, enjoyable alternative to your go-to donut option. That way, when you crave a breakfast donut, you can look forward to your healthier option.

Is there something that you try to do more on a superficial basis? Go to the gym? Eat healthy Wake up first? Kick a bad habit? Nobody trusts what your dreams are. It is an excellent deal of self-discipline, control, and knowing how to avoid temptation. Looking at the skills brilliantly, now you can improve your personal life and your work life. Here are ten recommendations so that you can pave the way to success.

1. Set a date

Research suggests that setting a start date to start an exchange in your existence can be an excellent ability to stick to your plan. Try to choose a day that is the first of the month, Monday, or the anniversary date of a year. Prohibiting a date is only a dream, so ensure that every intention also ends using the date.

2. Write down your reasons why you want to gain more self-discipline

Despite what many think, self-discipline is a discoverable behavior. It requires exercise and repetition in your day-to-day life. Focusing on greater values rather than immediate results can aid beef in self-control. Write high-quality notes for yourself every day and leave them in

the rooms you visit regularly.

3. Imagine the result of your efforts

Studies show that if you motivate yourself with excellent self-control results, then your self-discipline lasts longer. By trying something and then visualize yourself achieving that goal, you are preparing yourself to succeed.

4. What will you do when temptation comes?

An established power method is to draw a graph of what you say and do when you feel tempted. It is recognized as a self-regulation strategy.

5. Make it fun with the help of something you want to do

Studies show that by creating the proper habits, you can start by connecting what you like to do. It treats itself. When practicing self-control, it breaks, behaves, and rewards itself, especially itself. If you are dieting, designate Saturday as a cheat day. Trying to exercise more? Massage after a month's visit to the fitness center.

6. Get Rich Easy

It is necessary to get at least 6 hours of sleep every night; it will not be counted. Try to drink caffeine at least 4 hours before bedtime, not to interrupt your herbal sleep cycle.

7. Ask for help

Are your friends out for you when you have a feeling of temptation. Studies show that repeated reminders will help you to succeed. Also, some people may have an idea of what was done for them when it comes to self-discipline.

8. Weigh all your options

Making an impulsive choice can be the wrong choice, so make sure to weigh your choice more than before.

9. Avoid drinking alcohol

Alcohol can compromise the mind's strength by decreasing its capacity to effectively reflect any action's potential outcome. If alcohol is being served to you round-the-clock, try drinking a glass of water instead.

10. Being surrounded by people who like themselves

Studies show that undisciplined humans who want to do better tend toward more self-control humans. Together, they can be every other support system

By learning how to achieve self-discipline, you can begin the adjustments you desire to make. There are many ways to make this a habit, but the quality is the apparent reason you favor those matters in your lifestyle. When our motives are strong enough, we can achieve almost anything.

According to a 2013 study assisted by Wilhelm Hoffman, people with extreme self-control are happier than those without. It was found that this was real because self-disciplined subjects were additionally successful in dealing with objective conflicts.

These humans spent very little time arguing over whether or not to engage in behavior that was dangerous to their health and were in a position to make good choices extra easily. Self-disciplined no longer allowed her choice to be determined through impulses or emotions. Instead, they report on the ground every day rational selection, which is highly confusing or disturbing.

Besides, many may think self-discipline is a discovered behavior. It requires practice and repetition in your day-to-day life.

To improve your self-discipline, check out these five proven techniques to gain better control.

This routine will enhance your manipulation by establishing good habits, harming bad people, and making easy modifications to your everyday routine. Better self-discipline can help you make a nutritious choice, which is no longer emotional. Give it a shot. Your happiness will thank you for this.

Remove attachment Self-management is often the easiest when followed with the aid of the ancient saying, "out of sight, out of mind." While working to increase your self-discipline, removing all temptations and distractions from your environment is the best first step. If you are trying to manipulate your food more, then toss junk food. Ask your workplace intern to ask you to get away from the daily lunch order email. If you choose to improve your center of attention while working, flip your cell phone, and remove the clutter from your desk. If you're really in trouble, download the SelfControl app to block distracting websites - Facebook, YouTube, even email - for a set amount of time. Set yourself up for success by reducing the horrific effects.

2. Eat regularly and healthily. Studies have shown that low blood sugar regularly weakens a person's resolve.

When you are hungry, your hearing ability is affected because your intelligence is no longer functioning at its best possible capacity.

Hunger has made it difficult to concentrate on the duties at hand, no longer to make you grumpy and pessimistic. You are very much likely to have a weak sense of manipulation in all areas of our lifestyle - diet, exercise, work, relationships.... You name it. To stay on track, make sure you get well fueled with healthy snacks and ingredients every few hours for the day.

I make sure that I usually have some almond or mashed milk on hand. These snacks ensure that I can get healthy protein and a dose of fat during the day. Food often regulates your blood sugar levels and improves making your choices and abilities. Allow the talent to focus on your desires and preferences as your substitute for your growing belly.

3. Don't wait for it to "feel right," improve your self-discipline ability, improve your everyday routine, which can be uncomfortable and awkward.

Charles Duhig, the author of The Power of Habit, states that habitual behavior is traced to a phase of the genus known as the basal ganglia - the intelligence elements related to emotions, patterns, and memories.

On the other hand, decisions are made in the prefrontal cortex, an entirely distinct region. When a behavior becomes a habit, we stop using our decision-making skills but instead feature on auto-pilot.

Therefore, breaking a terrible habit and creating a new addiction not only requires us to make energetic decisions, but it will also look wrong. Your intelligence will alternatively cope with what has been done to do it. Solution?

Embrace the wrong. Accept that your new regime will take a little time to feel appropriate or over the top, or natural. Keep chugging along. This will happen.

Four schedule breaks, treats, and rewards for themselves. Self-discipline no longer allows your new routine to be utterly bloodless turkey, hardcore, or willing to drill like a sergeant in execution.

Giving up a room with their own zero frills often results in failures, disappointments, and historical ways. Working towards self-control, the timetable specifically breaks, behaves, and rewards itself. Dieting?

Designate Saturday as Ice Cream Sundae Day. Trying to lose weight? Treat yourself to a fancy massage after a month of gym visits. Were you working on controlling your expenses? Give yourself a $ 25 discount at the mall on Sunday. (Leave the savings card at home, and only take the money). Self-discipline can be difficult. Reward your effort

5. Forgive yourself and move on. You will have the ups and downs, appropriate successes and failures to provide a new way of thinking continuously as planned.

The key is to maintain further transfer. When you get a shock, it becomes famous what is happening and moves on.

It is easy to delve into guilt, anger, or frustration, although these feelings will not help improve self-discipline. Instead, use hiccups in your diagram as your experiences for the future. Forgive yourself, and return to the saddle ASAP. Now you are away from your game; it is hard going in a tremendous direction.

CHAPTER 3

Set transparent dreams and have an execution plan

According to "Expectancy Theory of Motivation," there should be three cases for a deeply and fully motivated character towards his goals.

If you have these three things, you will be drawn to something that excites you. You will have the self-confidence of a layout that you can execute. You usually make small wins, which turn into big wins.

Unstoppable Inspiration for 3 Needs

You must rely on a specific intention reward ('WHY'), meaningful and compelling.

You must believe that you understand (clear strategy/plan/ people) how to achieve your goal.

You must agree that you can implement the plans, strategies, and axes concerned with achieving the goal.

These are the massive three you have to succeed at any level. Interestingly, long before Expectancy Theory, billionaire H.W. L. Hunt said:

Decide exactly what you want and why

Your purpose or desired effect wants to be desirable. You need to wish it and have the intention to force it to try it.

Just as Jim Rohan said, "Reasons come. First, solutions come second." You want a reason to do something. Those reasons are your WHY.

The different purposes you can provide yourself to do something, the more motivated you will be. These causes, when powerful, form NEEDS. For example, look at your existence right now.

Most humans reveal their contemporary earnings as the product of their status or ability. Your current income is based on how much you trust.

If you need more, you will do more. If you wish to make an additional $ 50,000 in the subsequent six months due to the situation or demand for your goals, you will be surprised by what you can do. Necessity is the mother of invention.

Your current stage of profit reflects the measure of your cause. It is backward in most people. They work so they can make money. When you have compelling reasons, you earn cash so that you can do extra work. The work is sweet since you have unique and effective objectives for doing it.

If you can make your objectives more significant, extra exciting, and personally meaningful to you, you will start conceptualizing clear goals.

The bigger you are, the greater your needs. If you have huge goals, you will need more resources, a team of humans to help you, and potentially more income.

According to advertising legend Jay Abraham, there is a zero correlation between getting something right and making money. Many gifted human beings do not have enough motivation to take their work and lifestyle to the next level.

Although there is a zero relationship between being "good" and making money, there is a direct relationship between advertising and making money. Your reasons for achieving a specific goal are more and more compelling. Also, you will be ready to perform this word and succeed.

You cannot be motivated by being a clear imaginative, and presenter and objective for that vision. But to clarify that being innovative and presenter takes work and patience. It is exploring and asking yourself some tough questions.

Be clear on a vision that requires you to spend a lot of time going through things yourself and isolating yourself from all rounds of noise. A profoundly compelling WHY should be more than just prior success or "beating" various people.

You want to do something internally. You can increase the speed and speed of your success through external motivators. But the force used needs something very personal to you.

It doesn't count how big it is. You want to get as many data points from humans who have accomplished something similar. If anyone has achieved what you want to do, then you should test yourself. You are likely chasing another person's goal.

But equality with others should be expected. And you can use them as statistical factors to plot your course.

You cannot rely on your vision except for a thoughtful and strategic plan.

For example, if you intend to make 10 million dollars but have never made more than $ 50,000 per year, it does not depend on how attractive your intentions are; you cannot agree with all the possibilities.

You can speak excellently. But deep down, you will either be careless about yourself or be naive about the reality of your situation.

Being inexperienced is not a scary thing. But you want to be educated to accept that you can make something big. You want to reference what would be required, to be honest. And you also need to succeed in your goals in small ways.

2-3 years is sufficient time to make tremendous progress. In 2-3 years, you can become a millionaire. As Dean Graziosi once said, "I got 10 million through announcing yes, 'and I said,' No 'got a hundred million with help."

The clearer you are on your goal, the better the organization you will find solutions. A WHY is not enough. You want OW HOW's and WHO's to help you achieve that vision.

If you do not have technology and humans and sources or ways of obtaining resources, you will not be prompted and cannot achieve your goals.

If you have something that you owe entirely, it is your responsibility to place the game plan. Robin Sharma has said, "Better dream, extra essential for the team."

In the remarkable Book Scale or Fail, Allison, for example, provides the following 5 stage frameworks:

Step 1 - Inventor: You rule and run the domain. You are the domain. You create, sell, implement, and account for everything.

Stage 2 - The Venice: You have a handful of employees. However, you still start approving the entire lot coming in and out of your company.

Stage Three - The Ringleader: It can feel like a circus at times! You start building small groups (e.g., admin, customized service, marketing). At this stage, you are becoming clear on your vision without a doubt. You are leading crew meetings and creating systems and processes. You are very thin. People are still not clear about what their role is.

Step Four - CO-Producer: You start recruiting or promoting team leaders to address and brainstorm new ideas and opportunities. Your humans are just as imaginative and committed as you and start asking: How can we be proud of our customers?

How can we innovate? How can we increase revenue?

Stage 5 - Sports: In this stage of the game, they don't need you. You have super people who are dedicated and committed to the vision. You step out of the meetings again and stop offering your two cents. You let go every day and mainly focus on the giant picture.

It does not depend if you are an entrepreneur or not. This 5-step outline is very instructive.

At every stage, you need a new game plan. If you don't have a game plan going from Stage 1 to Stage 2, you won't get there.

Many humans think of themselves on stage 5 when they don't even understand how to get out of step 1 or 2.

Whatever your purpose, you want to strengthen a plan.

Techniques are needed to get you from where you want to go.

Once you climb to a positive level, you will need to redefine WHY - your purpose for what you are doing.

They have to rise big and high on the way because if it continues to increase, then the number of people in it will grow. This will affect a growing number of people through the work you do.

Without plans and people, you cannot be inspired. You cannot achieve big goals. You are being WHY is no longer enough. You need HOW and WHO, or as Dan Sullivan puts it, you want WHO to care.

According to the Hope Theory of Psychology, hope reflects your perceptions:

conceptualize goals

Develop precise strategies to reach those desires (i.e., thinking of the way)

Initiate and preserve motivation to implement these strategies

This theory is very comparable to the Expectancy Theory, which this entire article is wholly based on.

The idea is simple: you need an honestly defined purpose that is meaningful to you. Then you need to have clear plans and strategies to reach that goal.

You want to agree on the process (and people) that will work.

This leads us to this last factor - you need to accept it correctly.

If WHY is powerful, it does not depend if you do not have all the number of pleasant strategies.

If you do not believe you can execute, you will self-sabotage.

You want to agree on the plans and techniques you can develop. You want to consider that you can lead the mission - management is essential if you wish.

You must expand and develop your vision. And in fact, that is one of the main objectives for a significant imaginative and presenter - fundamentally transforming you into the kind of character who can do it.

Yes, you can expand and grow. You can strengthen your ability and skills. You can adapt to complex examples and do stuff that you didn't achieve before.

You can become comfortable in new and unknown areas.

You can become a person of confidence and trust who is willing to keep his stake in his land.

You reach this stage of investment, in which you invest by completing what you believe to be true.

You want to care enough about your desires to develop beyond your petty fears and self-image. You will need to get an accurate landing on marketing and leadership. You need to care enough about your imagination and presenter to study and how to reveal the message — as an alternative to the ultimate finale — an enthusiastic artist crammed with clear ideas about how other people are doing wrong things.

Whoever can conceive and believe can receive the thought. You may end up with additional resources than children.

You can pursue remarkably innovative and thoughtful and fun ideas and choices and dreams. As you develop through these dreams, you can develop into a great and beautiful person. As you diligently BECOME, learn, grow, lead, and share.

You are formidable and inspired. You have lofty intentions and dream big. You all know the importance of hard work to accomplish goals. Are you still continually falling for achieving your goals?

Do not blame yourself

Alternatively, focus on the targeting system. As a late American motivational speaker, Zig Ziggler said: "An objective superlative set has reached midway."

When setting your goals, pay attention to avoid these mistakes:

Error 1: Setting Indivisible Goals

In a 1981 study, Goal Setting and Task Performance: From 1969 to 1980, published in the journal Psychological Bulletin, a pioneer in goal-setting theory, Edwin A. Locke, stated, "Assessing both laboratory and field research on results. While doing assignments, fulfilling dreams found that specific and difficult dreams in 90% of studies lead to higher overall performance than easy goals. ' "Do your best or no goal."

The goals need to be clearly described. Imagine the stop result as if it had already happened.

for example...

Unclear Goal: I would like to make more money.

Specific goal: I want to increase my revenue by 50% within a year.

"My favorite word in intention setting and success, in general, is the word Clarity. Of course, you would accomplish the whole thing in life Brian Tracy, Chief Executive Officer of Training and Development Agency Brian Tracy International, in the Book, Goal! Writes: How to get everything you want - more than you ever thought possible.

To be specific, write your goals in detail.

Research indicates that writing their dreams helps them achieve them faster.

A 2007 study (unpublished but widely cited) with Gail Matthews, a psychology professor at Dominican University in the U.S., published that members who wrote their wishes were much higher than those who wrote them.

Writing brings readability to thought and tells you what you intend, and gives way to thoughts and actions.

Error 2: Dreaming while stopping the execution plan

After the successful invasion of Normandy in World War II, American time-honored Dwight D. Eisenhower requested the specific planning system that went into the charge, stating, "In preparation for war, I have generally found those plans to be useless, but the goal is inevitable. "

Even if you make specific goals, you will leave them in the middle of clear deadlines, lack of schedules, and the steps to achieve them. The plan for mini-targets and the daily pace was to bring it closer to its goal.

"The reason for planning enables you to transform your required precise objective into a planned, multi-task assignment with specific, specific steps," Tracy in Target writes!

Leo Babutata says, "A terrifying approach that I take a serious look at, most recently through the author of Simplicity: The Simple Science of Getting You Want, Mark Joyner, called Backward Planning.", Creator of Jane Habits - a weblog of finding ingenuity in the chaos of each day of our lives.

Here's how it works: Once you've defined the intention and its outcome, let's think about the final component you want to do to achieve that result.

Then what you want to do before that stage, and the scene before that, and so on, until you reach the first stage, the guardian. This is the step you need to pay attention to.

Error 3: setting too many goals

"You can do some work, but not everything now," product guide David Allen wrote in the ebook Making It All Work: Winning at the Game of Work and Business of Life.

If you make a long list addressing each area of personal life, and it is desirable to work in an alternative place, you are setting yourself up for failure.

In a 2012 study titled Many Good Things: Implementation Benefit Intentions depend on the number of goals published in the Journal of Consumer Research, Amy Dalton and Stephen Spiller determined that "when humans meet more than one goal Eliminates one, the enterprise's ability to ignore or postpone others, which reduces the perceived probability of meeting all goals The. "

A few well-defined desires allow you to focus on small action steps while keeping your energy focused, allowing you to make some distance extra effective. The same goes for the sub-goals that you have placed under each objective. If you have three significant wishes, but each has ten minis, it will not be possible to preserve the track and work continuously on all of them.

The key here is a handful of dreams you can remember.

According to Transform Your Habits creator James Clear, you have to choose an objective necessary for you and then set a schedule to work towards it consistently.

Successful desires are intelligent goals (specific, measurable, actionable, realistic, and time-bound).

Be smart when installing them, bend about the method of achieving them, and be consistent in your approach.

I would like to work a little, but ...

P. G. as Lord Havershet. Wodehouse's novel Laughing Gas says: "And bit by bit before you recognize the place you're in - why you are there, you don't know."

It is both simple and challenging. Simple because you just follow your plan. You are complicated because a lot of things get in the way. The critical thing to remember is that without action, your dreams will be dreams. Even if thoughts, ideas, and plans are necessary without doing anything, you will not realize your dream. Your thoughts will remain thoughts, and your goals will remain plans.

So what could happen between you and your goals:

Not enough time

You already have a busy schedule. Work is unpredictable, and sometimes it is too tiring to work on your goals after a day's work.

How can anyone blame you for just wanting to rest?

Is relaxation important?

If you have set a relevant goal, broke your destination for daily tasks, and tested your plan's feasibility, you really shouldn't have this problem.

Take a specific time each day to work on your plan. In the beginning, take the energy that you usually spend to make excuses and incorporate it into your plan at a specified time. Once you make a good habit, things get more comfortable.

Waiting for the right time

This will never be the right time. Get over it.

The same goes for waiting for the right people.

As you are executing your plan, you can find what your top priority is. When this happens, think about the result you want to achieve and make sure that your current daily work reflects essential tasks that will help achieve that result. If you have trouble making a decision, try one of these priority methods. It is difficult for those to prioritize because everything seems essential; check out this lifestyle article.

Lose interest

How many dreams are lost due to interest lost during execution?

Do the mental rehearsal of how it will be to achieve your goal. Engage all the senses. What will you see? Listen? Agree?

Expand your action in the future. Do you want it if you get what you are doing?

When they do not think they can achieve their goals, their interests diminish. If you are on a trust issue, read how always to achieve your goals.

Bonus!

I have mentioned this in Part One, but it is worth emphasizing.

What is going to make a difference is all the difference...

... get a pen and paper ready because it is essential...

In addition to tracking your daily progress (here is a free online habit tracker), ask yourself every week:

1. Am I able to work towards my goal every day? If not, what is happening in my way?

2. Is the goal still relevant to my vision and purpose? How is it relevant? Is this still the most impressive thing I can do to realize my dream?

3. Am I getting what I want from accomplishing this goal?

Write those answers down.

Once you reach your goal (note that I use "once" and "no"), reward yourself.

Once there is a clear, executable plan with properly aligned resources and capital, attention becomes paramount. More startups either wander off by focusing their attention on planning and objectives, chasing distracting shiny new objects, or get caught up in the minutiae and lose sight of overall goals and results. After building a great team and raising capital and maintaining the vision, and starting the plan, an early-stage entrepreneur / CEO's three most important tasks are.

Standard techniques to maintain focus are to publicly post-critical objectives and milestones, review milestones at the beginning of all hands-on meetings, tie bonuses or variable compensation to their achievement; And often overlooked, but perhaps most importantly, those milestones are essential to the state. People are far more willing to make the necessary sacrifices to pursue audacious goals, achieve extraordinary results, and deliver ground-breaking results when they understand why goals matter—explaining the "why" may be the most important thing you can do to achieve buy-in and co-ownership of goals.

Whether it is World Cup football or a startup team, it requires extraordinary effort to reach the top and deliver a stand-out performance. They are stating "why" is a crucial element of motivating team building. So is a shared sacrifice.

Although most of my work as CEO was between 7 am and 7 pm, I played 1 am foosball or improvised putt-putt games with the developers, who needed to blow off some steam because they wanted a release—used to pull an all-nighter to crank. And shared success and victory must come with shared sacrifice and shared rewards (a critical reason stock options are so crucial to Silicon Valley's success).

Celebrating company-wide wins in product development, sales, customer success, etc., was a key element to keep the team motivated at my startup.

Personalizing the customer was that the customer logo was prominently displayed on the reception area walls; even the new customers paid us that week.

Our daily workload often comes at us at a never-ending pace, and tasks are usually presented as immediate and necessary, but life is more than fighting the daily workload.

To achieve your dreams, you have to work on your plan and priorities instead of setting goals. The goal is the most critical part of the project, describing what you want to achieve. They also provide focus because once you have a clear purpose, you can rededicate yourself and confidently disregard ideas that do not contribute to your success.

Every person or organization must have a vision, a set of dreams, and big or bold long-term goals that provide a solid foundation for the goals you set. Your vision inspires and energizes you, guides you, and gives all efforts a purpose. It connects destinations to your deepest motivations and intent.

Many types of goals

Although not all goals are the same, some plans focus on results, while others focus more on performance.

Result goal

They focus on achieving something at a particular point in time, such as reading a specific book by the end of the month. If the goal is too large, divide it by year, quarter, month, and week. Outcome goals are harder to reach and, therefore, more frustrating if not achieved, but they also provide the most explicit and most important guidance.

Performance goal

Also known as performance goals, these goals focus on the tax side or the amount of time spent working on your plan. It plots activities done daily or weekly, such as reading for at least 5 minutes every day. It focuses on behavior and personal development that will lead you to a specific goal. Creating a routine that aligns with objectives rather than working directly on results allows many people to be even more successful.

And the benefits for this type of goal are plentiful: it creates habits when scoring regularly so that it sticks easily because patterns make complicated things more comfortable over time.

With this type of plan, you are also less likely to dissent because it is not binary. An 80% completion can still be considered an accomplishment; And an excess of results, such as 120%, can also be observed. An execution goal, i.e., going for a run every morning before work, a habit will be executed successfully while an outcome goal does not create a pattern; Either it is complete or not, i.e., to lose 10 pounds.

How to set your goal

Whether you choose the result or the execution, the key is to get down to patience and set some goals.

Step 1: Remember your vision and identify all possible goals associated with it. Think deeply. Again, goal setting is an essential step in planning. You are taking action backward first by separating the desired result from its execution, compared to collecting goals.

First, get Clarity on what you want to achieve. Then, find the best ways to get there. Targeting is not an easy task. Take your time and choose wisely. Be sure to include different aspects of both your business and life.

Some example questions to inspire you during this step:

What is your most important goal this year? This quarter? This month? Alternatively, what one thing do you want to achieve in the next 100 days?

When reviewing all that has worked well in the past, what are you doing or enhancing?

What can you do to improve your situation?

Can you stop doing something harmful to your vision and core values, your physical or financial health, relationships, and partnerships or happiness?

Think big and push yourself forward. There is a tendency to make goals as "realistic" and "possible" as possible.

This should be your starting point, but you should extend it further.

Get yourself out of your comfort zone. Feel confident that you can and will achieve your dreams.

Steve Jobs once said, "Everything around you is built by people no smarter than you." Isn't it encouraging? We all get what we consider deep inside.

Start with the end in mind. What is your desired result? Get to the root of why you want to achieve a goal. Have you identified one that is worth resolving? Do you want to solve it? Is this something you can do, or is it your strength?

Once you have decided, imagine your goal and all the actual benefits associated with reaching it.

The more personal it is, the better. The more you engage with each of your dreams, the more effort you will continue to make with all your efforts.

Step 2: Choose your most important goals for the upcoming period and work them out.

Choose some plans that you are committed to rather than doing what you think you should do.

Break any big goal into smaller goals. Most research supports the idea that setting short-term goals is more valuable than looking at the big picture. So it is better to break down goals into smaller monthly or weekly goals, even if you have an extensive list of long-term goals.

Be specific and clear. Be substantial Think about the particular things you want to start or achieve, not the goals. So instead, "Find happiness in life," try, "Be a loving and caring father." One way to check if your goal is clear enough is to ask yourself: How do I know when I have reached my goal? How do I measure success?

Step 3: Individual projects and action plans to reach this goal and at what time and by whom they have been done. Pay attention to what should be done. Every small achievement along the way will further boost your morale. Break down your goals into small individual steps such as those grouped by tasks, projects, or milestones. Professionals call this work breakdown structure.

Once established, now comes the classical discipline of project management. You are setting yourself up for action.

Planning is necessary, even though circumstances may change; while we have heard, "No war plan survives contact with the enemy," they also say, "the plan to thwart the plan is failing" and "You can always change your plan, but only if you have one.

What obstacles or challenges do you need to plan? At first glance, some may be obvious, but others may come in many different forms:

Confidence: When you have a belief that is preventing steady progress, write it down. Often when you find yourself saying such things as, "If I had ..." or, "If it were possible ..." - these are phrases to write. Once written, work to limit those beliefs. Get any positive evidence against them and think about how trust is formed in the first place. Sometimes the information you find while researching that particular belief will destroy it. At other times, you may have to create an event contrary to your previous experience to help limit trust.

Facts: Question the assumptions that we count as facts.

Arguing from "first principles," Elon Musk attempted to achieve the boldest goals with his rocket-launching and landing company SpaceX such as "reducing the cost of getting payloads into Earth orbit.

" To build a more affordable rocket from scratch, he chooses only to draw his conclusions from first principles, test any real-life assumptions, and continuously adjust his strategy through the learning process.

Habits: As human beings, we all create bad habits in life that may require re-deformation along the way. Think about those routines, subconscious things that can hinder your progress, i.e., eating late at night when your goal is to lose weight.

List all the beliefs, facts, and habits that prevent you from giving 100% to the goal.

The systems you design may be more important than the goals you set.

Pursuing only specific goals is difficult and risky. Instead, try to have as many performance goals as possible, of which you should regularly nail close to 100%.

For example, one of my performance goals that has quickly turned into a habit is my morning routine: Every other day, after getting up from bed and just before I go to work, I drink a book while drinking coffee.

Start with, then playing with my dog, and finally working on a personal and a professional activity that will make this day great. Another performance goal of mine is to complete at least ten items on my to-do list every week, no matter how small.

However, on an annual and quarterly basis, it is still essential to have some outcome goals. These goals will guide you while executing your plan. For example, I usually have a dream that I focus on each month and break it down into one or two weekly goals, with pre-planned tasks for each day. For all long-term goals, I keep a backlog of tasks grouped by projects I can pick up when there is more room to work or I'm blocked elsewhere.

A famous goal is to obtain wealth with many people. If you aim for this, first define a certain level of money you want to make and try to break it.

Divide your monetary goal by months and then by day and find out what kind of job or business can lead you to that level.

If you don't already have a number, start by counting the amount you need to have freedom or spending, which you can track your expenses using a notepad or spreadsheet.

However, we often settle for popular but unspecified goals, such as "I want to be a millionaire and retire." Apart from the lack of the above nuances, there are two problems with this:

People don't want to be millionaires - they only want to experience what they believe only millions of people can buy. However, research shows that people become happier as they make more and more money, but only up to about $ 70,000 per year. After that, marginal improvements experienced due to a higher income are usually offset by other factors such as stress, more hours, etc. When considering your monetary goal, consider doing all the things you want to do. Want, and not only buy everything. You want to have it.

Retirement as a goal assumes that you dislike that the retirement you are pursuing should not be a goal. Experience shows that the founders of businesses that sell their companies once become very bored, as they have shed cocktails on the beach for a few weeks. They then usually find their subsequent occupation because running a business is what they love and serve them as the purpose of being.

Then maybe reevaluate the goal of being a millionaire and retire. A reliable cash flow each day that offers freedom may be more necessary for your dream than winning millions in the lottery, if ever.

CPSIA information can be obtained
at www.ICGtesting.com
Printed in the USA
BVHW092008140521
607356BV00002B/32